My Ears Are Huge and Fuzzy

by Jessica Rudolph

Consultant:
Christopher Kuhar, PhD
Executive Director
Cleveland Metroparks Zoo
Cleveland, Ohio

BEARPORT
PUBLISHING

New York, New York

Credits

Cover, © Edwin Butter/Shutterstock; 4–5, © Zoltan Molna/Alamy Stock Photo; 6–7, © Edwin Butter/Shutterstock; 8–9, © oraveepix/Shutterstock; 10–11, © nattanan726/Shutterstock; 12–13, © vitovt/iStock; 14–15, © blickwinkel/Alamy Stock Photo; 16–17, © Konrad Wothe/Minden Pictures; 18–19, © Juniors Bildarchiv GmbH/Alamy Stock Photo; 20–21, © Juniors Bildarchiv GmbH/Alamy Stock Photo; 22, © Yossi Eshbol/Minden Pictures; 23, © Robert Eastman/Shutterstock; 24, © LifetimeStock/Shutterstock.

Publisher: Kenn Goin
Editor: J. Clark
Creative Director: Spencer Brinker
Design: Debrah Kaiser

Library of Congress Cataloging-in-Publication Data

Names: Rudolph, Jessica, author.
Title: My ears are huge and fuzzy / by Jessica Rudolph.
Description: New York, New York : Bearport Publishing, [2017] | Series: Zoo
    clues 2 | Audience: Ages 6–9._ | Includes bibliographical references and
    index.
Identifiers: LCCN 2016007667 (print) | LCCN 2016009511 (ebook) | ISBN
    9781944102579 (library binding) | ISBN 9781944102920 (ebook)
Subjects: LCSH: Fennec–Juvenile literature. | Foxes–Juvenile literature. |
    Zoo animals–Juvenile literature.
Classification: LCC QL737.C22 R78 2017 (print) | LCC QL737.C22 (ebook) | DDC
    599.776–dc23
LC record available at http://lccn.loc.gov/2016007667

For more information, write to Bearport Publishing Company, Inc., 45 West 21st Street, Suite 3B, New York, New York 10010. Printed in the United States of America.

10 9 8 7 6 5 4 3 2 1

Contents

What Am I?

Look at my fur.

It is soft and golden.

My eyes
are round
and dark.

6

I have four
paws.

8

Each one is very hairy.

My nose is black
and tiny.

10

11

My tail is fluffy.

It is dark brown
at the tip.

13

I have small,
white teeth.

14

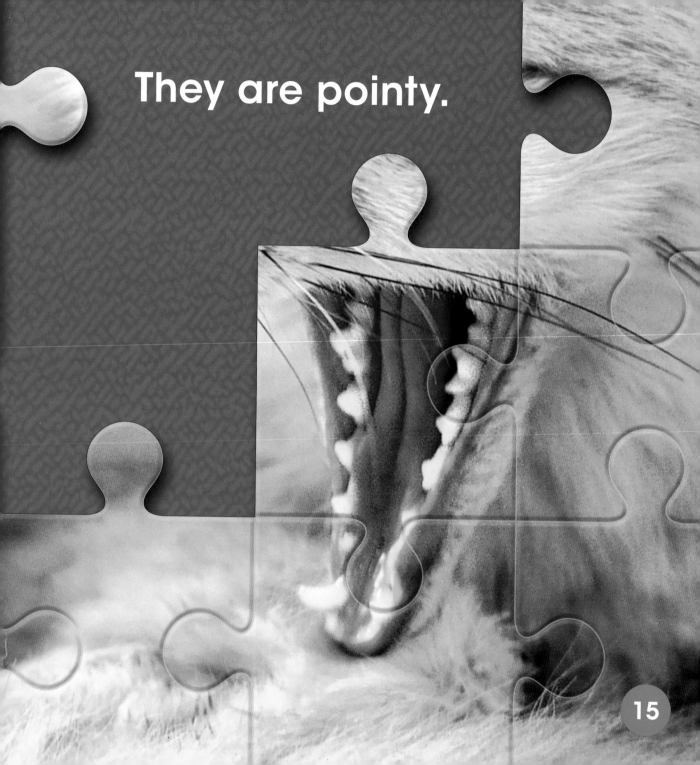

They are pointy.

My ears
are huge
and fuzzy.

16

17

What am I?

Let's find out!

I am a
fennec fox!

21

Animal Facts

The fennec fox is the smallest type of fox in the world. Like almost all mammals, fennec foxes give birth to live young that drink milk.

More Fennec Fox Facts

Food:	Plants, insects, and lizards
Size:	Up to 30 inches (76 cm) long, including the tail
Weight:	Up to 4 pounds (1.8 kg)
Life Span:	About 10 years in the wild
Cool Fact:	A fennec fox's big ears give off body heat. This helps the fox stay cool in the hot desert.

Adult Fennec
Fox Size

Where Do I Live?

Fennec foxes live mostly in the deserts of North Africa. They dig underground dens in the sandy soil.

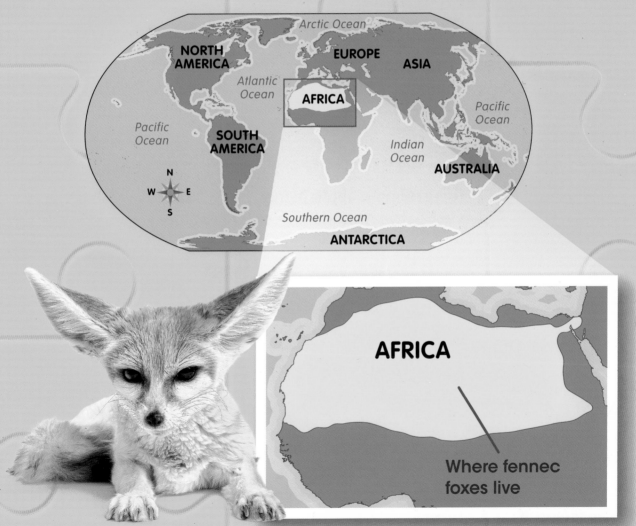

AFRICA

Where fennec foxes live

Index

Read More

Ganeri, Anita. *Fennec Fox (A Day in the Life: Desert Animals).* Chicago: Heinemann (2011).

Gardner, Jane P. *Fennec Foxes (Wild Canine Pups).* New York: Bearport (2014).

Learn More Online

To learn more about fennec foxes, visit
www.bearportpublishing.com/ZooClues

About the Author

Jessica Rudolph lives in Connecticut. She has edited and written many books about history, science, and nature for children.